FROM UNDER THE BRIDGE

By
Pamela Hillan & Penelope Dyan

Bellissima Publishing, LLC
Jamul, California
www.bellissimapublishing.com

Copyright © 2021 by Bellissima Publishing, LLC

Cover Photograph Public Domain by esudroff from, Pixabay

All rights reserved. No part of this book may be reproduced or transmitted in any form or by any means, electronic or mechanical, including any photocopying, or recording, or by any information or storage retrieval system, without permission from the publisher and author.

ISBN 978-1-61477-549-2
First Edition

"For our dearest Matthew with all our love"

About The Authors & The Book

Pamela Hillan and Penelope Dyan are lifelong friends who used to like to pretend they were in a Nancy Drew book when they were kids are back again, all grown up (and then some) they are still pretending! And this is why the Jan and Jenny books continue and why they began!

Penelope Dyan became a teacher, a published writer, a vocalist and a mother and an attorney, while Pamela Hillan became a mother and a court reporter . . . and then finally everything went back to what it was before all of that happened, and the Jan and Jenny books were born!

It was their combined lifelong experiences, and their great desire to do good in this world, along with their love for the law, and their deep concern for the homeless, that led to the creation of this latest book in the Jan and Jenny Mystery Series, that began with "The Mystery On Burgundy Street".

This is the fifteenth book in this series, and Jan and Jenny are out to save the world once again, as they begin a new adventure right at home. Jenny's Aunt Vi is by their side, and Ms. Wright and the Hufflefingers are helping the girls once again.

Take part in the excitement, as you travel through the pages of "From Under The Bridge", and find out what Jan and Jenny experienced, what they learned, and why what they did was so important.

FROM UNDER THE BRIDGE

By
Pamela Hillan & Penelope Dyan

From Under The Bridge

CHAPTER ONE

THE BOY AT HUFFLEFINGERS'

It had been some time since Jan and Jenny had been down to visit the Hufflefingers, and to be honest, the two of them were feeling a little guilty about that.

"It's been quite awhile since we walked down to the Hufflefingers' place," Jenny said, as she took a bite of warm brownie she and Jan had just pulled from the oven and lightly sprinkled with powdered sugar.

"Thanks for letting me have the corner piece," Jan said. "You know how much I like the chewy corners."

Jenny laughed.

"Well . . . what do you think?" Jenny asked. "I'm down here at your house now, and we can visit the horses down at the end of the road and easily walk over to the Hufflefingers' farm."

From Under The Bridge

"Well, it would be nice to see their pigeons again . . ." Jan began.

"And?" Jenny interrupted her.

"And the rabbits . . ." Jan continued.

"And?" Jenny interrupted again.

"And . . . the Hufflefingers, of course! I do hope they're both all right. They aren't getting any younger, after all," Jan finally added, to which Jenny nodded emphatically in agreement. "And it's been a long time since they were FBI agents."

"But they always end up helping us when we need them!" Jenny exclaimed.

"I'll bet they wish they could just retire in peace," Jan laughed, "but I guess once an agent for the FBI, always an agent for the FBI!"

And so this is how (most surprisingly) Jan and Jenny's latest adventure began. It was only supposed to be a simple visit to the Hufflefingers' house, and yet it turned into so much more. But, after all, nothing was ever quite that simple for Jan and Jenny.

So . . . after having their fill of milk and brownies, they cleaned up their mess and put everything away, and gave a shout out to Jan's mom that there were plenty of brownies left, and that they were heading out to visit the horses corralled at the end of the road, and then they would be off to visit the Hufflefingers!

"Give them our love!" Jan's mother shouted back at the two girls. "And I hope you cleaned up your mess!"

From Under The Bridge

"We did!" Jan shouted as the girls headed out the front door. "And there's enough brownies left for Cindy when she gets back from her friend's house . . . and enough brownies for dad too!"

"You girls be careful crossing that busy road!" Jan's mother shouted from the back room as the girls headed out the door.

Before they knew it, the two girls were sitting atop the corral fence petting the horses. A busload of young, Navy recruits drove by and started hooting and hollering at them, waving their arms.

"They must not know how young we are," Jenny said, as she waved back.

"Maybe they don't care," Jan told Jenny. "But we're safe enough. They can't do anything to us from that bus, and they're probably on their way to boot camp or something."

Jenny smiled.

"Probably," she said, as the girls jumped down from the corral fence and headed off to the Hufflefingers.

"I hate to visit empty handed," Jenny said. "Maybe we should have brought them some brownies."

"We are bringing them some brownies," Jan said, as she pointed back over her shoulder to the backpack on her back.

"I was wondering why you brought a backpack," Jenny told her. "But when did you do that? When did you pack the brownies?"

"Remember when you went to the bathroom?" Jan asked, raising her left eyebrow slightly. "I did it then."

"It's a good thing we made a triple batch, then," Jenny laughed.

Before they knew it, they were knocking on the Hufflefingers' front door; and to their surprise, a young boy opened the door and appeared in the doorway.

"Do the Hufflefingers still live here?" Jan asked wide-eyed.

"Oh, yeah," came the reply. "They're taking care of me right now."

He was a handsome Hispanic young boy, a bit younger than Jan and Jenny, with dark hair and beautiful, big brown eyes.

"Who is it, Matthew?" Mrs. Hufflefinger shouted from the kitchen.

"I don't know!" the young boy shouted back. "It's a couple of girls!"

"Oh, that must be Jan and Jenny!" Mrs. Hufflefinger shouted with excitement, as she wiped her hands on her apron.

Removing the apron, she headed out of the kitchen and shouted for Mr. Hufflefinger to join her.

"It's Jan and Jenny!" she shouted.

"I hope you packed enough brownies," Jenny whispered to Jan as the boy named Matthew turned to look at the now approaching Hufflefingers.

"Invite them inside," Mr. Hufflefinger said, as the young boy slowly and reluctantly opened the door and motioned the girls inside the small house.

From Under The Bridge

"This is Matthew," Mrs. Hufflefinger told the girls . "He's staying with us for a while."

"Nice to meet you, Matthew!" The girls said in unison.

"We brought brownies!" Jan added.

"I do love brownies!" Matthew told her, especially the corners.

"I think Jan probably ate all of those," Jenny laughed.

"Oh no, I didn't!" Jan exclaimed.

"Well, then you'll just have to fight Jan for them!" Jenny retorted, smiling.

"Wherever did you find this handsome young lad?" Jan then asked trying to appear much more grown up than she was.

"We found him under a bridge," Mr. Hufflefinger said, as they all walked toward the kitchen.

But that was only part of the story.

From Under The Bridge

CHAPTER TWO

LET'S GET SOME FACTS

Upon hearing that Matthew was found under a bridge, Jan's curiosity escalated to top priority. She knew there was an old bridge that went over the now empty San Diego River Basin that was located about a half mile from the Hufflefingers' property. And she knew that the police on several occasions had to clear out some homeless encampments that had settled in the old reeds that grew in place of the water that once stood there, close to the bridge. But she didn't know there were kids there.

What were you doing under the bridge, Matthew?" Jan asked in a calm, quiet voice, as the five of them sat drinking Mrs. Hufflefinger's fresh-squeezed lemonade and munching on the brownies Jan had stuffed into her backpack.

She could tell Matthew was quite shy and withdrawn.

From Under The Bridge

Upon hearing Jan's question, Matthew looked at Jan with tears in his eyes, put down the brownie he was eating, and walked away, going into the bedroom in which he was staying at the Hufflefingers'.

Jan felt terrible after she asked that question . . . and right off the bat. One of her problems was that she had a tendency to speak before thinking about what the consequences of her actions would bring.

"Oh, I'm so sorry," Jan said apologetically to Mr. and Mrs. Hufflefinger. "I should have known better."

Mrs. Hufflefinger walked over to Jan, who was seated in a kitchen chair, and patted her on the back.

Then she quietly responded by saying, "Oh, Jan, it's all right. We are just now learning that Matthew has been through a lot during his time on this earth, more than any child should ever have to endure. He is very fragile at this point, but we are trying to show him that there are good people in this world that want to help him. It's been a slow process, but in the three months he's been here, we are starting to see him relax a little and open up to us more."

Then Mr. Hufflefinger interrupted, saying, "Yes, he is. You know, I found him under that old bridge by the dried-up riverbed. He was half starving to death. He had bruises over fifty percent of his body. He was like a scared animal. It took quite a bit of coaxing just to get him to come out in the open. But he was so hungry, and cold, and dirty. I guess he figured I looked like an OK guy, so he decided to come back home with me."

Jan and Jenny both had big alligator tears in their eyes after hearing Matthew's story, or at least part of it. They realized how lucky they were to have both a mother and father who loved them very much and took care of them every day of their lives.

Is there anything we can do to help?" Jenny asked with sincerity in her voice, as Jan nodded her head in agreement.

"The best thing to do right now is to just take it slowly," Mr. Hufflefinger answered. "Why don't you girls come by this weekend and we all can take a little hike or something. Matthew should feel better by then."

Jan realized that was probably their cue to leave, since she had upset Matthew; so both girls got up from their chairs, said their good-byes to the Hufflefingers; and as they walked out the door they called out to Matthew, "Good-bye, Matthew! Nice to meet you. See you later!"

"Thanks for the brownies!" Matthew called out after them from his bedroom.

And they then walked back to Jan's house, talking about how they could make Matthew feel better about things. They decided if Matthew had some real friends, perhaps he would feel better about things. Perhaps he would even feel better about everything. Only time would tell, and the girls were out to do their best to welcome this frightened young boy into their world.

"I only hope it's true that time heals all wounds," Jenny said, as they turned the corner and walked up the sidewalk to Jan's house.

"So do I," Jan told her, thoughtfully. "So do I."

CHAPTER THREE

More About Matthew

Just as the girls walked in the front door, Jenny's cell phone rang. It was Ms. Wright. Jenny wondered why Ms. Wright was calling, but Jan (being Jan) knew why Ms. Wright was calling immediately.

"She talked to the Hufflefingers," Jan said, as Jenny looked somewhat puzzled.

"This is Jenny," Jenny announced, answering her cell phone.

"I heard you met Matthew," Ms. Wright, the familiar voice that was an attorney for the FBI, and who was also a longtime friend of the Hufflefingers, and now the girls, began.

"Yes, we did," Jenny said, as she put her cell phone on speaker, and the two girls sat down on the living room couch.

From Under The Bridge

"Then you know Mr. Hufflefinger found him under a bridge, and that he is in desperate need of friends."

"We kind of figured that out," Jan said, chiming into the conversation.

"Hello, Jan," Ms. Wright said. "I was hoping to talk to you two when you were together. And you are together, so this is good."

"Can you tell us more about Matthew?" Jan asked. "He became very upset when I asked him why he was living under a bridge. I don't want to upset him again."

"Matthew and his brother were abandoned by his mother. It seems they were living under that bridge, and then their mother took them to the nearby sheriff's office, said she would be right back, and then left them there standing at the sheriff's door. When the sheriff's deputy opened the door to answer a call, Matthew hid in the bushes, and told his younger brother not to say anything about him being there, because he was going to find their mother. So, the sheriff's deputy was able to reunite Jeffery with his father, but Matthew went running back to the bridge to look for their mother."

"I don't quite understand," Jenny told Ms. Wright. "Why couldn't Matthew go with Jeffery to their father?"

"They have different fathers; and Matthew's father was abusive to him and didn't want him in his life, because he had married another woman and was fighting paternity."

"Fighting paternity?" Jenny asked. "What about DNA?"

From Under The Bridge

"There's the law, and then there's Texas," Ms. Wright explained. "Matthew's father moved to Texas. And there was really no point in placing Matthew with an abusive father."

"That makes sense," Jan interjected, as Jenny silently nodded her head in agreement.

"But how did you get involved in all of this?" Jenny asked.

"The Hufflefingers called me after Mr. Hufflefinger brought Matthew into their home," Ms. Wright explained. "And since we are longtime old friends, I intervened with the Sheriff's office and got them a temporary guardianship through the court so they could take care of Matthew, as well as with any emergencies that might arise. They love Matthew; and they are very patient people, so this was a perfect fit."

"They're wonderful, generous people," Jenny told Ms. Wright, to which Ms. Wright wholeheartedly agreed!

"What about his mother?" Jan asked.

"His mother is a drug addict," Ms. Wright then told the girls. "And she is in bed with the Mexican drug cartel as well. Her children just got in the way of her perverse life."

"Her perverse life?" Jenny asked. "Besides the drug thing, how was her life perverse?"

"It seems she sold herself for money to buy drugs, and she sold Matthew as well. Jeffery was lucky. No one wanted to buy him, and I guess she also figured he was too young; and he fought back and screamed at the top of his lungs for help every single time she tried it. Matthew, on the other hand, put up with it."

"But why?" Jenny asked.

"It's simple. He loved his mother. He would do anything for his mother."

"It's too bad the feeling wasn't mutual," Jan said, as tears began to stream down her cheeks.

"Addiction to drugs is a terrible thing!" Ms. Wright told the girls.

"What can we do to help . . . besides being good friends to Matthew?" Jan asked.

And that was how (and when) it all began.

But now it was time for dinner. And Jan's mother was calling them all to dinner. After that, Jenny would head for home. Her mother had agreed to pick her up after work, so she didn't have to take that long uphill walk back to her house. And that pleased Jenny, because the Hufflefinger visit had been emotionally exhausting, and now she just wanted to curl up on her bed and read a good book. Of course, she would probably do her homework first.

CHAPTER FOUR

Google, Google

The next day, while Jan was sitting on her bed doing a google search, she came across some interesting statistics for abused children. She felt that Jenny needed to know these things immediately, so she picked up her cell phone and called her best friend.

Jenny just happened to be sitting in her bedroom on her own bed, doing the exact same thing Jan was! Jan and Jenny were so much alike when it came to their thought processes. It was uncanny, really.

Jenny noticed her cell phone vibrating on her bedside next to her. She had her phone on mute so she wouldn't disturb her dad, who slept during the day most of the time, because he played lead trumpet in a band during the evening at various venues. He was a fantastic trumpeter! And he was an overall great musician too!

From Under The Bridge

Jenny reached for her phone, seeing on her screen that it was Jan calling.

"Hello there," Jenny said quietly. "What's up?"

Jan, excited to tell Jenny what she had learned from her search, quickly exclaimed, "A lot is up! I've been researching abused kids and it's just unbelievable!

Before Jan could get another word out of her mouth, Jenny interrupted her.

"Great minds think alike," she said. "I've been doing my own research! You're right, though. This is the saddest thing I've learned about in a very long time. I had no idea!"

Then, Jan quoted a statistic and said, "Did you know 'A report of child abuse or rape is made every ten seconds in the United States!' And that 1,809 deaths were reported in 2019 from child abuse!"

Almost in tears at this point, Jan sobbingly added, "I'll bet it was a lot more in 2020 with Covid going on and with kids quarantined with their abusers! We need to do something about this, Jenny!"

"We really do!" Jenny replied, with commitment in her voice. "And did you know that the United States has one of the worst records among industrialized nations for abused children?"

"OMG!" Jan shrieked. "How could this happen in our country, Jenny? It makes me sick to my stomach just thinking about it!"

Jenny was thinking about poor Matthew.

From Under The Bridge

"I can't even imagine what poor Matthew must have been going through all these years. It must really mess with your mind to be tortured like that . . . don't you think?"

Disgusted with the facts just presented, Jan replied, "I can't think! I'm just appalled that this is happening in our country at all! There must be something we can do, Jenny! Maybe Ms. Wright knows how we can help."

"Jan, are you reading my mind again?" Jenny asked. "That's exactly what I was about to say!

"Why don't you come over and spend the night? It's a weekend, so maybe we can devise a plan. I did my homework last night, " Jenny told her.

"I did mine too!" Jan exclaimed. "I wanted to get it out of the way. Besides, I didn't have very much, and it was easy."

"Then it's a go?" Jenny asked.

"I'll ask my mom," Jan replied. "I'm sure my parents would like some alone time. My sister is staying with a friend for the weekend, so that would be perfect! But what about Matthew? Aren't we supposed to go down to the Hufflefingers?"

"Just get the okay from your mom, Jan. We will figure out the rest. I promise!"

And Jan and Jenny were once again devising a plan to save the world . . . or at least to help some abused kids, even if the only one they ended up helping turned out to be Matthew!

CHAPTER FIVE

WHAT CAN WE DO?

Jan's mom gave the okay for Jan to spend the weekend with Jenny, and even drove her up to Jenny's house. She didn't like the idea of Jan going anywhere alone now and advised her to always stay in groups of two or more when she did anything or went anywhere, because if there were at least two people doing something, like walking down the street, and someone tried to grab one of them, the other one could scream and run for help.

That all made sense to Jan, and she decided not to ever argue with her mother about that; because she actually realized (especially now) how lucky she was to have a mother who really, truly loved her. And she told her mother exactly that.

"Is this because of that young boy, Matthew?" her mother asked as she drove Jan up to Jenny's house.

"Not exactly," Jan told her. "I've always been grateful to you for being such a great mom. It's just that after being with Matthew, I realize how very grateful I am."

Jan's mother smiled as she pulled into Jenny's driveway.

"Please don't you two get into any trouble," she told Jan, knowing how the girls were prone to such things.

"I won't," Jan told her; but she made no promises.

It seemed like trouble always seemed to find the girls; but so far they'd always managed to come out of their adventures unscathed.

"Don't go 'Nancy Drew' on me again," her mother told her, as she grabbed her overnight bag from the back seat, shut the car's doors, and headed up to the front door of Jenny's house.

"I'll try not to!" Jan shouted back, being quite truthful with her mother.

Jan's mother put the car into reverse and backed out of the driveway pondering over why she had ever purchased those books for Jan. But as she headed home, she finally decided that reading those mystery stories probably didn't actually have a great deal to do with Jan and Jenny's penchant for adventure and for helping others, because it was simply their nature to help and to do what they thought needed to be done. Jan's mom was also grateful the Hufflefingers and Ms. Wright seemed to always have their eyes on the two girls.

So . . . as the two girls sat on Jenny's bed, they researched on their laptops, and they tried to figure out what they could do.

From Under The Bridge

Jenny's Aunt Vi came into the room and wondered what the girls were up to now, and Jenny told her all about Matthew, and how he had lived under a bridge, and how they wanted to fix things for abused children.

"You can't save the entire world," Jenny's Aunt Vi told them. "You really can't!"

"But we can try," Jenny told her. "Some kids just don't have what we have, and just maybe they need some help."

"What do you have in mind?" Jenny's Aunt Vi then asked.

"We can start by bringing them some food!" Jan exclaimed. "Maybe we can gain their trust. We won't bring them money, just some food, and maybe some juice packets or something."

"Now, that's an idea!" Jenny's Aunt Vi exclaimed.

"And we can be a good friend to Matthew," Jan added, to which Jenny agreed.

"But you shouldn't go down there alone," Jenny's Aunt Vi told them. "I'll go with you."

The girls smiled at what seemed to be a good and safe idea.

"Maybe we can get some other kids to help too! Maybe we can get some kids from the church youth group to help!" Jenny exclaimed.

"I don't think you want to overwhelm them if you are trying to earn their trust," Jenny's Aunt Vi told the girls. "One step at a time is how this should be done."

From Under The Bridge

"Well, we promised to visit Matthew today," Jenny told her Aunt Vi. "Maybe we can all go down to the bridge after that. I'm sure it will be a short visit."

And so, the plan was set in motion. It was only the first part of the plan, and the three of them were determined to make a go of this thing, as they took apples and bread and peanut butter and whatever they could find from the cupboard to bring down to the children under the bridge.

Jenny's Aunt Vi drove them down to visit the Hufflefingers so the girls could spend some time with Matthew, which they did, as Jenny's Aunt Vi visited with the Hufflefingers and told them about the girls' plan.

"We're glad they're not doing this alone," Mrs. Hufflefinger said. "I'm afraid it could be dangerous under that bridge."

"That's why I'm going with them," Jenny's Aunt Vi told Mrs. Hufflefinger."

And shortly thereafter, Jenny's Aunt Vi drove them as close to the bridge where Mr. Hufflefinger had found Matthew as they could get, and she parked the car. Then they grabbed the three bags of groceries they'd scavenged from the cupboards at Jenny's house, each carrying one bag; and the three of them headed for the bridge (after first locking the car for safety's sake).

From Under The Bridge

Jenny's Aunt Vi was quite nervous about doing this, but she knew the girls were determined to do this and that it would be much safer if they had a responsible adult with them.

To Jenny's Aunt Vi's great relief, as they were handing out the food to the kids (who were now all smiles) Ms. Wright came walking toward them.

From Under The Bridge

CHAPTER SIX

AN ISSUE OF TRUST

Jan and Jenny were starting to get the small group of kids under the bridge to let down their guard. Jenny's Aunt Vi stood off from the group to observe, but not look intrusive. The children were so hungry that not much talking took place, only the scarfing down of every morsel of food they were given, as well as the variety of boxed drinks that were supplied. The girls saw no adults whatsoever and wondered where they all were.

Suddenly, the children saw Ms. Wright in her three-piece pinstriped suit and high heels approaching them, and they all ran away and scattered in different directions, afraid that she was there to take them away!

Jan, seeing the kids fleeing, called for them to stop.

From Under The Bridge

"Hey, kids! It's okay!" Jan shouted. "She's a friend of ours, and she only wants to help!"

However, the children were nowhere to be found at this point, even after Jan and Jenny, and Vi and Ms. Wright did a cursory search of the area.

"I suppose they hid in the underbrush," Ms. Wright said, sighing.

Disappointed, Jan had to offer her two cents worth.

"Boy, they sure are good at hiding," Jan said. "And they're so fast! And just when I thought they were warming up to us."

"I just wanted to talk to them," Ms. Wright told the girls. "I should have let you two earn their trust first. This is apparently a terrible situation that may take some time to remedy. We need to rethink how we should handle this. Let's go to the Hufflefinger's house and try and speak with Matthew," she said, as she turned and walked toward Jenny's Aunt Vi, and the two of them walked up the hill to their cars.

"Okay" Jan mumbled, looking at Jenny. "We'll just leave this food and drinks over in the shaded area. The way they were scarfing this stuff down, I'm sure they will be back for more."

Jenny helped Jan carry the bags of what was still left of the food and boxed drinks over to the shade under the bridge.

Whispering to Jenny, Jan said, "I like Ms. Wright, but she should have known better than to show up at our first attempt to talk to these poor kids. And she shouldn't have worn a three-piece pinstriped suit and high heels."

Jenny, nodding her head in agreement, whispered back, "I know. But she was probably coming from court, or something. I know she's trying to protect and help us, but we should ask her to wait for us to learn more about what's going on with these kids."

After placing the food where they were sure the kids would find it, they headed back to the street where Jenny's Aunt Vi and Ms. Wright were now standing next to their cars having a discussion.

Arriving back at the vehicles, Jan and Jenny opened the car door belonging to Aunt Vi, without speaking a word.

Jenny's Aunt Vi, seeing Jan and Jenny were not in the best of moods, apologized for their behavior to Ms. Wright.

Ms. Wright, realizing she had made a mistake by coming, replied, "That sounds like the best idea for now."

As she walked past Vi's car to get to hers, she waved at Jan and Jenny and said, "We'll talk when we all get back to the Hufflefingers' place. I'm sorry if I ruined your plans."

Jan and Jenny waved back at Ms. Wright, and in an attempt to be cordial, and quickly getting over their now fleeting disappointment, Jan rolled down the car window and (after getting the okay from Jenny's Aunt Vi) suggested they all go get something to eat at Nicolosis' Italian Restaurant before they went to visit Matthew.

From Under The Bridge

Ms. Wright smiled and gave an okay signal to the girls, very much relieved the girls had suggested she join them. She was quite familiar with the restaurant, which wasn't too far away from where they were now; and it was close to lunchtime.

As Jenny's Aunt Vi got into the driver's seat and started the engine, Ms. Wright drove away, heading in the direction of the restaurant.

It was going to be a very interesting lunch. Jenny could feel it in her bones.

"You have that look again," Jan said.

"What look?" Jenny asked.

"You know . . . the knowing thing look," Jan told her.

And Jenny smiled. She did feel like they were on the brink of something good, something very, very good!

CHAPTER SEVEN

LET THEM EAT PIZZA!

When they got to Nicolosis' and were seated, Ms. Wright opened the conversation with yet another apology. The waiter, who happened to be the owners' son, couldn't help but overhear the conversation, and he quickly assessed the problem and went to talk to his father (who just also happened to be a friend of Jenny's father).

When he came back with their sodas and torpedo sandwiches, all placed on a big round tray, he said, "I couldn't help but overhear what you were saying about the kids under the bridge."

Jan and Jenny watched as he set the food and drinks in front of each of them, and they wondered what he was going to say next. Ms. Wright and Jenny's Aunt Vi said nothing and just looked up at the waiter, wide-eyed.

From Under The Bridge

"I talked to my dad," the waiter told the four of them. "And we want to help. We'd like to deliver them some pizzas . . . on the house, of course."

"How marvelous!" Ms. Wright exclaimed. "I wonder if we can get other businesses to pitch in and help as well."

"I don't know about anyone else, but it does seem like a good thing to do," the waiter told Ms. Wright.

"One step at a time," Jenny's Aunt Vi said with a huge smile on her face.

"How many pizzas will you need?" the waiter asked.

"Is ten too many?" Jan asked in return.

"Sounds fine to me, "Are pepperoni and cheese pizzas okay?"

"Perfect!" the girls replied in unison.

"Is tomorrow at this time okay for the pick-up?" the waiter then asked.

Jenny looked at her Aunt Vi for confirmation.

"I'm at your service," she said.

And so, it was all settled!

"By the way, my name is Salvatore, but you can call me Sam. And since my dad is friends with Jenny's dad, your meal this afternoon is on the house! So be sure to order some spumoni for dessert!"

The girls were beside themselves! What luck. They might not be able to change the entire world, but maybe they could actually help those kids under the bridge!

From Under The Bridge

"Now, don't get ahead of yourselves," Ms. Wright warned them, very much aware of the ways of the world. "This is only the beginning. And we will all do what we can do, whether it is a little or a lot."

And then they ate their meal, and had their spumoni, and got in their respective cars and drove off to the Hufflefingers! And Ms. Write promised to wear jeans and cowboy boots and a plaid red, flannel shirt and to stay back in the distance with Jenny's Aunt Vi when they delivered the pizzas after church the next day.

"For once, they'll have something to eat on Sunday!" Jan exclaimed.

"And there's nothing quite like pizza!" Jenny added.

Jenny couldn't wait to tell her dad all about it!

"Well, I was right," Jan said to Jenny as they exited the car at the Hufflefingers house and Ms. Wright pulled her car up behind them on the street and parked.

"What do you mean?" Jenny asked.

"The knowing thing!" Jan told her. "I knew you knew something good was going to happen, and it did!"

"Maybe you have a knowing thing too, Jan. After all, you knew that I knew something good was going to happen!"

After that, the girls both laughed as the three of them headed toward the door of the Hufflefingers' home, joined by Ms. Wright.

"Kick me if I say something stupid or go too far with Matthew," Jan whispered to Jenny, as the door opened and the three of them and Ms. Wright were invited inside the house.

And this time, Ms. Wright had put on her flats, and she had taken off her vest and jacket so as to not intimidate anyone. (But actually, the truth was she was very, very hot, and her feet hurt. After all, Matthew and the Hufflefingers had already seen her in her three-piece pinstriped suit and high heels, so it had nothing at all to do with being intimidating, because they hadn't been intimidated at all by her attire on her first visit that had occurred earlier that day.)

CHAPTER EIGHT

Matthew's Out Of His shell

Once inside the Hufflefinger's residence, everyone was escorted into the family room where there was adequate seating for everyone.

Mrs. Hufflefinger walked into the kitchen to get refreshments, while Mr. Hufflefinger called out for Matthew to come into the family room to have a chat.

To Jan and Jenny's surprise, Matthew didn't have to be coaxed to join the group. This time he seemed much more at ease, even smiling when he came in and sat down, greeting everyone with a pleasant "Hello."

Jan and Jenny, both smiling happily, greeted Matthew with their "Hi, Matthew," as well.

From Under The Bridge

Mr. Hufflefinger started off the conversation by asking Jan and Jenny how their attempt went to communicate with the kids under the bridge.

Jan glanced at Ms. Wright, while replying, "Oh, it could have gone better. But at least we were able to give them some food and boxed fruit drinks. They seemed very hungry."

Then Jenny interrupted Jan by saying, "I thought they looked malnourished and very dirty. Those kids need help desperately, but I think they are afraid of being taken away to some horrible place and forgotten."

Then Matthew stood up by his chair and said, "A lot of them have at least one parent living under the bridge with them, or close to it, in a homeless encampment further down, by the dry riverbed. The kids go where you saw them to play."

Ms. Wright then interjected an interesting piece of information.

"Well, unfortunately, due to a limited budget from the county, many of the hospitals housing the mentally challenged and drug addicted adults have been forced to release them to go out on their own and fend for themselves. Often, once released, they have children that they sadly have responsibility for as well. And their children are released to them from their foster homes where they were safe and well fed, simply because the biological parent makes a case before the court to get them back, saying they are well now and were released from the hospital. It's a very sad situation and one that definitely needs to be revised. These individuals can barely take care of themselves, let alone any children they may have. But if they have children, they get money from welfare, and that's their true incentive in getting their kids back, because with money they can buy drugs. And many think they are self medicating. It's a disgrace, really, that our own government is allowing this to happen. And I'm trying my best to get more attention drawn to this issue so it can somehow be resolved."

"My mom is a drug addict," Matthew then announced, with tears welling up in his eyes.

He was trying to be strong and not cry. He was so thankful that the Hufflefingers had taken him into their home; but there were so many more kids that had no one to help them, and they were just wandering around trying to stay alive any way they could.

"My mom was released from the hospital, because they didn't have any more room for her. There were patients worse off than she was, so she was released. I love her, but she's very sick. She does bad things to get her drugs. I know she doesn't mean to be bad and hurt me, but the drugs have control over her, and she tells me she can't help it. That's why I'm happy the Hufflefingers are helping me. She was making me do bad things too, so she could get her fix!" Then Matthew broke down. It was finally too much for him to say, and he couldn't continue.

Everyone in the room felt Matthew's pain and had tears in their eyes as well.

Just then, Mrs. Hufflefinger entered the room with a large tray of goodies, announcing, "Anyone for drinks and snacks?" That lightened up the atmosphere a bit, and everyone helped themselves to the delicious tray of homemade banana bread, brownies, and milk or lemonade to wash it all down. This was the perfect time for a break! It didn't matter that they had eaten their fill at lunch. It was the perfect social break.

CHAPTER NINE

Matthew Wants To Come

After a while, Matthew went to his room to think about some things. His heart was crying out to him. He knew what he had to do. He listened as the girls told the Hufflefingers about the pizza they would be bringing to the kids under the bridge the next day, and as the girls and Jenny's Aunt Vi and Ms. Wright were getting up to leave, he entered the room.

"I want to go with you tomorrow," he said. "Is that okay?" he politely asked, turning his attention to the Hufflefingers.

"I suppose so," Mrs. Hufflefinger told him.

"I think it's a splendid idea," Ms. Wright interjected, thinking not only would it be helpful in establishing trust, but it just might help Matthew fight his demons.

"We're getting the pizzas right after church," Jan interjected. "Can you be ready at about one o'clock?"

"Sure!" Matthew told Jan.

"Should we come as well?" Mrs. Hufflefinger asked.

"I don't think so," Ms. Wright told her. "We don't want to overwhelm the kids like I did earlier today. But Matthew will definitely be an asset in this in establishing that trust we need."

"Will it be dangerous?" Mrs. Hufflefinger asked.

"I certainly hope not," Ms. Wright said, as Jenny's Aunt Vi stood silent and wide-eyed and as Mr. Hufflefinger remained silent as well. "But I will definitely have agents on standby and ready to intervene if necessary."

"That sounds about right to me," Mr. Hufflefinger told her; "because I do fear that no good deed goes unpunished."

Mrs. Hufflefinger shook her head and said, "Now, now, Mr. Hufflefinger, let's have positive thoughts about this . . ."

After that everyone said their good-byes, and they were all off with anticipation and excitement rising over the expectations for the next day.

"It's sad that in 1980 the Mental Health Systems Act was signed by then President Jimmy Carter, that provided grants to mental health systems, and then in 1981 when Ronald Reagan was president, he and the US congress repealed most of the law, especially since the Mental Health Systems Act was considered to be landmark legislation for mental health," Jenny's Aunt Vi told them as they headed toward Jenny's house in her car.

"Oh my!" Jan exclaimed. "Do people even realize what happened? Do they understand what that caused?"

"It actually began with Reagan in California when he was governor here," Jenny's Aunt Vi added. "Since the number of patients had fallen, he used that to cut funding to mental institutions. And it was President John F. Kennedy who signed the Community Health Act to put the Feds in charge to establish community health centers and take some of the onus from the states. But then he was assassinated less than a month later, and the community health centers never received stable funding."

"How do you know all of that?" Jenny asked.

"Well . . . I'm not the only one in the family who knows how to use Google," Jenny's Aunt Vi told her. "And there's even more, but I'll let you girls look up that history firsthand."

"Something needs to be done! Something needs to be done!" Jan said, shaking her head. "This is so wrong! Something bad will happen!"

"Bad things are already happening," Jenny's Aunt Vi told the girls.

"But what can we do?" Jenny asked.

"You need to simply keep being you! Speak the truth! Stand up for what is right! You are, after all, the future; and the future is, after all, yours!" Jenny's Aunt Vi told them.

From Under The Bridge

After that, the girls sat in silence, each thinking about Matthew and about what was happening right here in the greatest country in the world. They knew in their hearts that if they didn't become a part of the solution, they would be a part of the problem. And that was that! And tomorrow would be another day!

From Under The Bridge

CHAPTER TEN

PIZZA TIME!

The following day, after a good night's sleep at their respective homes, and after church, and after picking up the ten promised pizza's, everyone met up once again at the Hufflefingers' house to basically strategize.

The plan was for Jan, Jenny, and Matthew to take the pizzas down to the children staying under the bridge while Jenny's Aunt Vi and Ms. Wright stood a respectable distance away in the background. Since Matthew was already a familiar face among a few of the homeless kids that were there, Jan, Jenny and Matthew were accepted readily by the children, which pleased Jan and Jenny very much.

As the pizzas were being passed out to everyone present, Jenny sensed an uncomfortable vibe amongst the kids. Matthew felt it too.

From Under The Bridge

"What's going on, guys?" Matthew asked with deep concern.

One of the older girls there, Kayla, who was probably close to twelve years old, answered with a frightened look on her face, "Jimmy never came back last night. No one knows what happened to him."

She then took a big bite of pizza, chewing and swallowing it as fast as she could. It was obvious she was very hungry! It was almost as if she thought someone might take the food right out of her mouth!

"Isn't Jimmy one of the kids that was doing stuff for Mr. Carter, the drug guy?" Matthew asked her.

Kayla took another bite of pizza and as she chewed it she half covered her mouth in order to be polite and said, "Yes. And he's not the only one that has gone missing lately. We think Mr. Carter is doing something to them or with them, and a few of us heard Jimmy and Mr. Carter arguing just before he disappeared, and Jimmy seemed really scared after that."

Matthew glanced at Jan and Jenny, who were both looking bewildered as they absorbed Kayla's comments.

Jan walked closer to Kayla, and with a look of concern timidly asked, "And where is this Mr. Carter now, Kayla?"

Kayla shook her head, indicating she didn't really know.

"He's a very mean man, you know. He makes all of us do bad things for him. He told us if we don't do what he says that we will be sorry. So, we really don't have any choice but to follow his orders. I think he might have hurt Jimmy."

After telling the girls that, Kayla started sobbing; and Matthew went over to her and put his arms around her to console her.

Jenny was next to ask a question of Kayla, once Kayla had gained her composure.

"Do you know where we might find this Mr. Carter? Maybe it would be easier for us to just ask him where Jimmy went."

Then a boy named Mark, who was around age fifteen, offered some additional information.

"I know he hangs out around Fairmount and El Cajon Boulevard sometimes," he said. "He's asked me to meet him there at the card room on the corner."

Jan asked Mark if he could describe this nefarious Mr. Carter to them.

"Gee, I don't know," Mark began. "I guess he's about 5'9", 150 pounds, kinda skinny actually. He has black greasy hair, slicked back. He has a tattoo of a snake going around his neck. I think he's Asian, but I'm not sure. He usually is dressed in black. That's about it."

Jenny, being quite impressed with the description given, exclaimed, "That's a great description, Mark! You did good!"

"I did?" Mark replied questioningly, as if he wasn't used to ever receiving any kind of praise.

From Under The Bridge

In fact, most of the children Jan and Jenny had met so far seemed like really good kids, who had just been placed in an unfortunate situation through no fault of their own. The more time they spent with them, the more Jan and Jenny felt they just had to help these kids out . . . somehow . . . some way.

But where should they begin?

CHAPTER ELEVEN

THE GREAT ESCAPE!

Much to everyone's surprise, Jimmy suddenly came hobbling up to the gathered crowd of kids.

"Jimmy!" Kayla shouted, as she ran towards him.

Jimmy could barely walk.

"I escaped," he said. "A dog saved me! He chewed off the ropes!" he said, quite out of breath, as though it took everything inside of his young body just to talk.

A large German Shepherd dog came out from behind some bushes and immediately ran to Jimmy's side.

"I call him, Shep," Jimmy told Kayla in a soft, worn, scratchy voice. "I yelled and yelled for help. Shep was the only one who heard me. I was tied up and thrown into that old sewage drain down by the

From Under The Bridge

river. I thought I was gong to die!" Jimmy said as he stumbled along with Kayla holding him up, helping him to walk.

"Come get some pizza!" Matthew shouted as another young girl ran to help Kayla with Jimmy, who could barely walk now, because he was so tired.

"Maybe we should sit down here," the girl who had come to join them offered.

"No," Jimmy told her. "I have to keep going. I have to get away from here."

As the three of them arrived to where the rest of the kids were standing and sitting and eating pizza, and downing juice boxes, the girl who had gone to help Kayla quickly explained the situation.

"He tried to kill me," Jimmy told the group of kids. "And if he finds me he will kill me! I know way too much! I know where he hides out. I know what he does with the kids who disappear."

Upon hearing that, Jenny took her cell phone and quickly called Ms. Wright.

"We have a situation," Jenny told her. "We need an ambulance and some protection!"

"Without even asking for details, Ms. Wright immediately contacted an ambulance and the agents she had on standby.

"I hear you," she said. "Help is on the way!"

From Under The Bridge

Jimmy was so tired, beaten, and stressed that he couldn't even eat. Ms. Wright ran down to where everyone was, this time not dressed in threatening attire.

"It's okay," Jan told the kids. "She's here to help you . . . all of you. And trust me. She's a good friend, and she will!"

"I won't go anywhere unless Shep can go with me," Jimmy told Jan and Jenny.

"Don't worry. I'll take care of Shep myself," Jan told him. And when you are all better, he can be with you again."

"You are a very brave and courageous boy," Jenny told him as the ambulance arrived at the street and the paramedics came running toward the group with a folded stretcher.

"Thank-you," Jimmy said, as he was put on the stretcher and carried up to the ambulance.

Ms. Wright stayed behind and watched as Shep followed the stretcher and Jimmy being carried up the hill by the paramedics. Instinctively, Jenny's Aunt Vi put the dog into her car.

Jimmy smiled and said thank-you, as they put him into an ambulance where an agent was waiting to further protect the young lad.

"I'll protect you now,' the agent told Jimmy. "I promise to keep you safe," he added, as an IV saline solution was readied and placed into Jimmy's arm. "You'll feel better soon. I promise," the agent told him.

From Under The Bridge

And then the agent told Jimmy his own story, which was not unlike what had happened to Jimmy.

Jimmy finally felt safe, but he knew the other kids were still in danger. He was too exhausted to tell his story, but said to the agent, "I will tell you everything."

And then, because he was completely exhausted, he fell fast asleep.

CHAPTER TWELVE

THE STOLEN SCHOOL BUS

While all of this intervention with Jimmy was taking place by the old bridge, in another part of town, not too far away, evil Mr. Carter was making plans of his own.

When he went to retrieve Jimmy from where he had left him in the old sewer drain, and realized Jimmy had somehow escaped, that was the last straw! The kids were disrupting his plans, and he needed to fix things once and for all! In his mind, all of the kids were losers! Most of their parents were strung out on drugs and heroin, which he happened to be supplying to them in exchange for committing crimes for him to prosper in his own right . . . burglary, robbery, car theft, et cetera. He figured that the kids of these so-called parents were doomed from the beginning. And he reasoned that

From Under The Bridge

nobody really cared about them or would even miss them . . . but he was completely wrong!

Back at the river basin by the old bridge, things were wrapping up for the day. Ms. Wright was going to look into individual care immediately for the homeless children, and Matthew was going back to the Hufflefingers where the three of them would await further instructions. And Jan and Jenny told the kids, numbering around fourteen, that they were going to do everything possible to help them and their parents, who had set up camp further down the river's basin, and to hold tight and to not worry. The girls promised that they would return the following day with more food and with more help. At least that was the plan.

Much later that evening, after everyone involved now had returned to their own homes for the night, the kids under the bridge, all huddled together to keep warm, heard the sound of a vehicle approaching from what previously had been an unused road for many years. They huddled closer to one another, wondering what was happening. They heard the engine of the approaching vehicle stop running. They were very frightened and very scared!

Suddenly, they heard heavy footsteps, and a bright flashlight turned in their direction as a gruff voice yelled out, "Come on, kids. We are going to a better place where you will be warm! I've got a bus parked over on the old fire access road here. Come on now! Let's get going!"

From Under The Bridge

It was Mr. Carter! He'd stolen a bus from the schoolyard parking lot, right from under the nose of the bus driver, who had been gone for only a few minutes so he could use the bathroom.

Mr. Carter was moving the kids to an unknown location, assuring them that they would be warm and well cared for. The children thought anything was better than the conditions where they were living. So, they all got up, brushed off the dirt from their shabby clothing, and followed Mr. Carter to the stolen bus. Once they were all piled in and seated, Mr. Carter sat in the driver's seat and drove them away. He didn't say where they were going.

What he had forgotten about was the school bus driver, who had immediately reported the bus as stolen from the school parking lot. And what was even worse for Mr. Carter was that he had now committed the federal crime of kidnapping. You see, someone did care, and that was what Mr. Carter had never expected.

The next morning, bright and early, Jan and Jenny, and Aunt Vi, drove back down to the Hufflefingers. Since it was a school holiday, Presidents' Day, time was not an issue They had all planned to meet there with Ms. Wright to continue strategizing a plan for the children and their parents (that is, the few that did have parents there in the vicinity with them). Jan's dad had cooked up a bunch of breakfast burritos for Jan and Jenny to distribute to everyone, and they stopped at Jan's house along the way to pick them up for the kids. And since there were fourteen or so kids, that was a lot of burritos! But being in the Navy previously, Jan's dad had experience feeding larger groups of people on a regular basis.

They parked in front of the Hufflefingers' house, left the burritos in the car, rang the doorbell, and were ushered inside by Mr. Hufflefinger.

When Ms. Wright arrived, shortly thereafter, they all exchanged notes on their progress before heading down to the bridge to feed the kids and hopefully give them some great news! They had no idea what had happened!

Jenny suddenly had one of her knowing things.

"Something is wrong!" Jenny suddenly told the others. " I can feel it!"

She looked very pale and had to sit down.

"What's wrong, Jenny?" Jan asked, worried now; because she knew that look on Jenny's face! "We better get down to those kids pronto! I think this might be serious!"

Everyone in the room jumped up to leave, including the Hufflefingers and Matthew, all hoping Jenny was wrong about the prediction she'd just announced!

They drove down the hill to the bridge in the two vehicles, speeding all the way. Once parked, they got out of the cars and yelled for the kids to come out, saying they had breakfast burritos waiting for them that were nice and warm. No one came out from under the bridge. No one was at the grassy area next to the bridge. It was eerily quiet!

Jan ran over to the bridge. All she saw was some dirty rumpled up blankets and a lot of garbage laying around on the dirt.

Gasping in horror, she yelled back to the others, "The kids are gone! All of them!"

Jenny cried out, "Dear Lord, please keep them safe!" And then she quickly added, "We've got to find them! What happened?"

Then Ms. Wright got on her phone and called for a search party to come to their location. She was told about the school bus theft, and figured out that it had to be Mr. Carter who had taken the bus to abscond with the children.

Don't worry," Ms. Wright told everyone as she finished her call, trying to calm everyone down. "Help is on the way! We will get to the bottom of this! Don't you worry!"

But . . . that was easier said than done!

Ms. Wright was furious that this had happened! She felt bad that the children had been essentially kidnapped on her watch.

Then the adults appeared looking for their children, and they were frantic. In spite of everything, and in spite of their addictions, and their homelessness, and their inability to properly care for their children, the majority of them loved those they had brought into the world and simply thought the world had given them a raw deal.

And then the federal agents arrived, right on cue. They'd coordinated with the Sheriff's Department, who had the information on the stolen school bus. And if they were lucky, it would just be a matter of time before the school bus and the kids were located.

CHAPTER THIRTEEN

JIMMY BLOWS THE WHISTLE

Meanwhile, Jimmy had awakened at the hospital, and while he was still very weak, he was anxious to tell the agent who was guarding him everything that he knew about Mr. Carter.

It seemed there was an old, abandoned warehouse in the downtown area, into which Mr. Carter had moved his drug business. He'd kept several of the missing, older children there to work for him preparing various drugs and whatnot on the black market. There were a couple of guards there, guarding the entrance from the inside, and two windows facing the street that were also guarded. All the guards were manned with high-powered rifles of some sort.

Of course, this information was immediately related to Ms. Wright, who was now strategizing with several agents and several sheriff's deputies on site.

From Under The Bridge

Since there were cameras posted on stoplights downtown, they were able to ascertain the exact path the school bus had taken. The only problem came when Mr. Carter abandoned the school bus and made the children walk to their final destination.

However, this turned out to be yet another error on the part of Mr. Carter, because two of the older children, one of them Kayla, had managed to run away for help, figuring out that Mr. Carter was up to no good as far as the kids were concerned. In fact, Kayla had been wondering why they were all so stupid. Why in the world had they gotten on that school bus in the first place?

Because Mr. Carter was forced to keep his eye on the remining twelve children, he couldn't go running after the two that ran away from him, and if he shot at them with the automatic pistol he carried in his pocket, it would generate too much attention. Where he was taking them, blocks away, was the only abandoned warehouse in the area at the moment; and he felt it was a good choice, because he paid no rent, so no one knew he and his illicit operation were even there!

They arrived at the warehouse; and the children, minus the two escapees, were ushered inside the building. The kids were excited to see the faces of the kids who had been missing from the riverbed. But they had no idea what terror lay ahead of them.

There was even a bomb in the building, rigged and ready to go off in case of trouble. And now the evil Mr. Carter had twelve additional young hostages!

From Under The Bridge

It didn't take long to trace Mr. Carter's steps and location. Matthew was a huge help and was able to confirm what Jimmy had told the agent at the hospital, which was a great help, and enabled Ms. Wright to get an emergency search warrant issued . . . just in case it was needed.

Suddenly, from outside the warehouse, sirens sounded. Lights from police vehicles and sheriff's vehicles began flashing. And the FBI agents arrived in unmarked cars.

"Come out with your hands up," came the voice from a police car's loudspeaker.

"I have armed guards, a bomb at the ready, and twelve hostages I am ready to sacrifice one at a time unless my demands are met!" Mr. Carter shouted back from where he stood at the window next to one of his armed guards, as he held a young child in his arms. "I'll start with this child!" he shouted. "And I'll throw her lifeless body out of this window unless my demands are met!"

Ms. Wright, search warrant in hand, called the principal players over to where she was standing next to her car.

"It's time to call in the hostage negotiators," she said. "This guy means business, and right now he has nothing to lose."

CHAPTER FOURTEEN

Meanwhile

Back at the Hufflefingers', Jan and Jenny, and Jenny's Aunt Vi, and Matthew and the Hufflefingers were sitting in the proverbial huddle trying to figure out what they should do next. Matthew was visibly upset.

"You don't understand just how bad that guy is," Matthew told them. "I mean . . . he's really bad. He really is bad . . ."

Mrs. Hufflefinger shook her head in despair.

"It's a crying shame," she said. "It's a darn crying shame. And I thought I had just about seen it all."

Jenny's Aunt Vi said nothing as Mr. Hufflefinger spoke.

"Well, Ms. Wright will handle this," he said. "She's not only a great attorney, she's also a very fine FBI agent. And she has a lot of support."

From Under The Bridge

Jenny, unable to keep herself from speaking, blurted out, "She'll need it!"

This caused Matthew to retreat to his room.

"I'm sorry," Jenny told the Hufflefingers. "I didn't mean to say that. It just sort of came out."

"Don't worry about it, my dear. Matthew has had such a difficult time," she said And then she added, "Did you know that Jimmy will be coming to live with us for awhile!"

"You'll have a houseful!" Jenny's Aunt Vi told her hesitantly, because (after all) two disturbed children in one house was indeed a lot for an older couple the age of the Hufflefingers to take on comfortably.

As if reading Jenny's Aunt Vi's mind, Mrs. Hufflefinger said, "I'm rather looking forward to welcoming Jimmy into our home. It gives us something to do! And when you're surrounded by young people, it helps you stay young!"

Jenny's Aunt Vi nodded her head in agreement.

"When do you expect Jimmy to arrive here?" she asked.

"Well," Mrs. Hufflefinger told her, "I suppose when this thing is all cleared up with Mr. Carter and the kids. I do hope those children are safe."

"I think we all would agree that we want those children to be safe," Mr. Hufflefinger said, to which everyone agreed.

From Under The Bridge

Mrs. Hufflefinger then walked from the living room where they'd been huddling and went into the kitchen to fetch a plate of fresh chocolate chip cookies she'd baked earlier that day.

"Can I help you with anything?" Jan asked, after Mrs. Hufflefinger had announced where she was off to and why. "I do love chocolate chip cookies! And you do make the very best chocolate chip cookies!"

"How about helping me with the paper cups and the pitcher of lemonade?" Mrs. Hufflefinger asked Jan.

"I have a much better idea!" Mr. Hufflefinger exclaimed. "Let's all go and sit down at the kitchen table!"

"That's a wonderful idea!" Mrs. Hufflefinger replied excitedly. "We can make this a party, of sorts. Heaven knows that we all need a bit of cheering up around here!"

"Did someone say party?" Matthew asked, as he reentered the room. "And did I hear something about lemonade and cookies?"

"You sure did, buddy," Mr. Hufflefinger said, as he got up and went over to Matthew and tousled Matthew's dark hair.

Matthew laughed. It felt good to be wanted and loved all at the same time.

Just as they were getting seated at the table, Jenny's phone rang. It was Ms. Wright. Jenny put the phone on speaker mode.

"I'm calling to update you," Ms. Wright said.

Jenny couldn't help but to wonder if this would be the end of the party, and that worried her.

"I hope the children are all right," Mrs. Hufflefinger said.

"Now, now . . . let's not get ahead of ourselves, Mrs. Hufflefinger," Mr. Hufflefinger told her. "All good things take their time."

Jenny, being the pessimist, wasn't quite sure that was true, and so she waited for the update before deciding.

"The children are fine so far," Ms. Wright began. "We have a hostage negotiator here, and it looks like Mr. Carter is in the mood to make a deal, seeing as he is far, far outnumbered."

"I don't understand," Mr. Hufflefinger mumbled. "I don't understand."

"Right now, you don't need to understand," Ms. Wright said. "I just wanted to give you a short update."

"But where are you?" Mrs. Hufflefinger asked.

"That's not important either," Ms. Wright said. "We have a strong coalition here, and I do believe we have the upper hand here. But this will take time, maybe far into the night! And I promise to update all of you as things develop if it is feasible to do so."

Jan and Jenny said nothing.

"Take good care of the girls and Matthew," she said, obviously directing this comment to Jenny's Aunt Vi and the Hufflefingers."

"What do you think she meant by that?" Jan whispered to Jenny.

"I have no idea," Jenny whispered back.

"Well, I have to go now. I'm sorry to cut you off, but one of the agents needs me to confer with him."

And then Ms. Wright ended the conversation rather abruptly.

"Do you think we're safe?" Jan asked the Hufflefingers.

"You forget," Mr. Hufflefinger told her. "Mrs. Hufflefinger and I are both retired FBI agents! Of course, you're safe."

That seemed to calm Jan down a bit. She imagined that the Hufflefingers had an arsenal of weapons somewhere in the house that they were not afraid to use.

However, Jenny remained a bit skeptical. She needed more facts about what was happening, and she hated being left in the dark about anything.

"Maybe I've been hanging around Jan for too long," she chuckled to herself. "But . . . after all . . . this is rather exciting."

CHAPTER FIFTEEN

LET'S MAKE A DEAL

Ms. Wright was right when she told everyone at the Hufflefingers that negotiations would take quite a while. In fact, the negotiator in charge had been trying to reason with Mr. Carter for over four hours by the time she had called them. The children being held hostage were hungry, thirsty, and scared to death.

Mr. Carter had been racking his brain trying to figure out how he could maybe get out of this mess without getting killed. The more he thought about it, after listening to the negotiator offering suggestions for surrender and possible leniency in sentencing, or even immunity if he was able to expose others who were doing the same thing, or worse, he was giving serious consideration to the idea of ratting out a few people he wanted to see out of the picture. Yes, that sounded like the best route for him to take.

From Under The Bridge

"I want to speak to that lady in charge! I want to talk to Ms. Wright! And I want to speak to her right now!" he demanded.

He was yelling out the window at the top of his lungs!

Then Mr. Carter screamed, "I'll let these kids go if you send her in here right now!"

He kept demanding.

"Send in Ms. Wright!" he shouted out the left side front window, "or I'll throw out the body of one of these kiddies instead!"

After that, there was a lot of commotion and arguing among those in the negotiating tent that had been set up when the stand-off first started.

Ms. Wright, who was seated in the tent, agreed to go in and talk to Carter, even though she was advised against it, because no one really knew what this guy was actually capable of doing.

Speaking confidently, Ms. Wright disagreed with all of them.

"No. I'm going in there," she said " I think this guy is just one of the little players. I'm afraid the ladder goes a lot higher than Mr. Carter. Maybe we can even get to the top of the ladder if we play our cards right!"

Ms. Wright secured a bullet-proof vest under her shirt and put her FBI jacket on top of that. She told the lead negotiator to tell Mr. Carter to release the kids and that she was coming into the warehouse as soon as the children were all safely released.

From Under The Bridge

The lead negotiator did as he was told, and speaking over the police loudspeaker, the negotiator announced "Mr. Carter, Ms. Wright has agreed to come in and speak with you, but first you must release all of the children. You have five minutes to release the children."

Upon hearing that announcement over the loudspeaker, Mr. Carter gathered the kids and told them to stand by the front entrance to the warehouse. They were crying. Some were screaming, afraid of what he was going to do. Mr. Carter looked out the side front window once more and saw Ms. Wright standing in plain view about fifty feet away from the front entrance, waiting for the children to come out.

Then Mr. Carter opened the front door and shoved one of the kids outside.

"Go on! Get out of here," he yelled, turning back to look at the rest of the children. "All of you get out now!"

At that point the children went running and screaming toward the police vehicles, hoping they would finally have protection, and they were greeted with open arms and warm blankets, and immediately taken to a secure location in a nearby hotel.

Ms. Wright was relieved that part of the negotiation was finished. Now it was time to hear what this guy had in mind to save himself, if that was even possible! She slowly walked toward the entrance to the building, gun in hand.

From Under The Bridge

"I'm coming in now, Mr. Carter," she said as calmly as she possibly could. "Open the door and stand back, with your hands in the air and in plain view," she announced in a loud voice.

"I'm unarmed!" he shouted, "and I'm being compliant!"

As she entered the building, Mr. Carter did as she requested. She frisked him, still holding gun in hand, told him to sit in one of the chairs sitting next to a close-by table, and she did the same. He was not armed. His armed guards, knowing this was now a lost cause, put down their rifles (and without having to be told or coaxed) headed out the entrance door, hands in the air, and were quickly cuffed, arrested, and taken into custody, ready to immediately turn state's evidence against whomever they could to gain their own promises of leniency.

The mood was extremely tense inside the warehouse and only Mr. Carter and Ms. Wright remained . . . but as they continued to talk, things calmed down. They talked for over two hours. Ms. Wright wore a hidden mike so her team on the outside knew she was safe, and things were going well. She also recorded everything on a shoulder cam she had on the shoulder of her jacket. She was careful to get everything in writing and signed by Mr. Carter. And for good measure, and because she was also a sworn federal agent, she read him his rights before they began.

She and Mr. Carter only came to a tentative agreement, after the second hour of grueling negotiation. Then came the signed writing.

From Under The Bridge

He agreed that he would turn state's evidence in exchange for leniency in his sentencing, and that he would plead guilty to a lessor offense, as he had intended to do all along (once the odds were piled so high against him that he saw no way out) to which Ms. Wright was also able to offer as well as to agree, since she was the attorney for the FBI, and a sworn agent, and also because this was essentially a federal case. As they were getting ready to go out the door, with Carter in handcuffs at this point, Carter turned in Ms. Wright's direction and began to speak.

"You know, who I'm giving you is only a drop in the bucket. There are millions out there much worse than I ever was. You will never catch all of them! They are way too smart for the likes of any law enforcement officers, even the FBI! Mark my words, lady! You will lose. You will *always* lose."

"And I suppose you would like to negate this deal?" Ms. Wright asked. "The deal we just made is dependent on your full and truthful cooperation, and you need to remember that!"

Mr. Carter turned an ashen grey and mumbled something about the 'worthless' children he had just set free. He'd forgotten that he'd signed and dated a written agreement, and that he'd been read his rights before the negotiations began.

After that, Ms. Wright didn't say another word. Carter's words sent chills down her back!

From Under The Bridge

As they walked over to the negotiator's tent, her gun drawn and pointed at his back, his hands high in the air, she said, "Get this guy out of here! Take him into custody, and get him out of my face!"

Mr. Carter was ushered out of the negotiator's tent by an agent for the FBI, and as he and the federal agent left, he was told, "You are under arrest. You have the right to remain silent. You have the right to an attorney. If you can't afford an attorney, one will be provided to you at no cost."

"Does that mean my agreement is no good?" Mr. Carter asked.

"That all depends," he was told.

"Depends on what?" he asked.

"It all depends on how you look at it," the agent told him.

"Get me an attorney!" Mr. Carter demanded.

Then Ms. Wright sat down in a close-by chair, put her face in her hands, and wept, and mumbled over and over again, "God help us. God help us one and all!"

CHAPTER SIXTEEN

WHEN THINGS GO RIGHT

Jenny's phone rang. It was Ms. Wright calling, and Jenny had been beside herself with worry since the last call from her, as was everyone else who was at the Hufflefingers. In fact, Jan and Jenny were actually afraid to leave; although Jenny's Aunt Vi (as usual) remained calm.

"This is Jenny," Jenny said as she put her phone in speaker mode so everyone could hear.

"It's time to relax and celebrate!" Ms. Wright said in a rather celebratory voice; because it was indeed a time to celebrate, even though there was still a great deal to be resolved.

"Celebrate? Really?" Jan asked in disbelief. "Tell us what happened!"

From Under The Bridge

"The children are all safe and at a hotel, all except for Jimmy and Matthew . . . and you know where they are! And the best news is Mr. Carter has turned state's evidence. And . . . he is now in federal custody."

"What did you have to promise him to get that?" Jenny asked.

"It's not important," Ms. Wright told her. "The important thing is we're getting a handle on this thing, and after an exhausting day, I am now recovering as you all should. You are safe. We've got names. We're readying the troops for further arrests, and for you the work is just about done . . . even though for me the work is just beginning."

"Oh my," Mrs. Hufflefinger said. "I can imagine."

"I know you can," Ms. Wright told her. "But I'm excited about it, and I'm getting my second wind now. And I want to apologize for not calling sooner, but everything was quite overwhelming; and I just needed to catch my breath."

"I understand, dear," Mrs. Hufflefinger told her.

"I know you do," Ms. Wright replied. "And I want to tell Jan and Jenny and Matthew and Jimmy that this couldn't have happened without them."

"But I didn't do anything," Matthew interjected. "You helped more than you realize," Ms. Wright said. "What you told us confirmed Jimmy's story and that's exactly what we needed for the search warrant."

"The search warrant?" Jenny asked. "Is that how you found the kids?"

"Not exactly. I will fill you in as soon as I am able. Everything must be kept quite hush, hush at the moment so we can continue to round up the others and not arouse suspicion."

"Others? What others? Are there more?" Jan asked innocently believing this was the end of the road as far as this was concerned.

"There are always others," Ms. Wright told her. "And so for now you must remain mum about this and not say anything. I promise to fill you all in as soon as I am able, just like I said."

"Life is never dull when Jan and Jenny happen to be around," Mr. Hufflefinger quipped.

"That's for sure!" Matthew added.

"Is Jimmy there yet?" Ms. Wright asked.

"Not yet. I expect he might be by later, but we shall see . . . or maybe tomorrow," Mrs. Hufflefinger said; and then she apologized for dominating the conversation.

"Nonsense!" Ms. Wright told her. "It's always a pleasure talking to you!"

"Would you like to stop by for dinner?" Mrs. Hufflefinger asked. "I'm making my famous meatloaf with broccoli and mashed potatoes and I have an apple pie at the ready for dessert!"

"As wonderful as that sounds, I'm afraid I will be working well into the night on this case, but I promise to stop by your place soon, as soon as things settle down with this case. I'll have hearings in the morning, and if not, at least in the next day or two. There's so much to be done."

"We understand," Mr. Hufflefinger told Ms. Wright.

"Now, don't you feel like you're obligated or anything like that," Mrs. Hufflefinger told her.

"Oh, I never feel obligated," Ms. Wright told her. "I only feel welcome!"

Mr. and Mrs. Hufflefinger both smiled at hearing that, and Mr. Hufflefinger quickly added, "Oh, and by the way, Shep is settling in here just fine!"

"That's wonderful, so wonderful. Jimmy was so worried he'd never see the pooch that saved him again!"

"He's a great dog!" Matthew said. "And he's a very brave dog too!"

"Just like all you kids!" Ms. Wright told them. "I hope I have a dozen just like you!"

And with that the call was ended, because Ms. Wright was called out of the negotiator's temporary tent to follow up with the bomb squad . . . she hoped without incident. And then there was the issue with the parents of the children. They also needed care. They were just as much victims as were their children. And while they might *never* fully recover, their children still loved them no matter what, so something had to be done. If America believed in family values, it was actually very simple. America had to stop thinking of the addicted, poor and homeless people, as people against whom war should be wrought, and they needed to start thinking about the poor, homeless and addicted as people they should help and heal!

And as to this issue, every single child and every single parent of a child deserved a chance to grow strong and heal.

And Jan and Jenny knew this, and this is why they were so determined to make this wrong into a right!

CHAPTER SEVENTEEN

EXHAUSTION

Everyone at the Hufflefinger's felt a deep sense of relief upon hearing that the children under the bridge were being taken care of and were well. Even though Jan and Jenny and the others at the house were mostly just sitting around and waiting while all the excitement was unfolding elsewhere, it created a lot of stress and anxiety for them just the same, not knowing what the outcome was going to be. The stress and tension build-up were indeed real! And now it was time for a good night's sleep, not to mention the fact that the weekend was over, and school was once again back in session for Jan and Jenny beginning bright and early in the morning, too early as far as the two girls were concerned.

Jenny was reluctant to bring the subject of the time to the rest of the crew, but it was absolutely necessary, and so she began.

From Under The Bridge

She started the conversation off by saying, "Jan, guess what time it is?"

Jan looked at Jenny, knowing the next words out of her mouth were probably going to be something she didn't want to hear. Jan was so tired already that she could barely muster up saying, "What time is that, Jenny?"

Breaking the bad news, Jenny said with a grimacing look, "It's time to go home, get some sleep, and get back to school bright and early tomorrow morning!"

Jan, nodding her head in agreement, slowly rose from her seated position, grabbed her backpack and the lightweight jacket she had brought, and started heading for the door, saying her good-byes to the Hufflefingers and Matthew. Jenny followed Jan to the door, while explaining to everyone there why they had to leave. And of course, Jenny's Aunt Vi followed behind the girls, apologizing for them and for the abrupt departure.

Mrs. Hufflefinger, understanding the girls' schedule, replied, "No need for apologies! Tomorrow is another day! We will keep you updated on any further progress that takes place in this case, girls," she added, now directing her comments to Jan and Jenny. "Have a good night's sleep, and a great week of educational enlightenment at school!"

Then Mrs. Hufflefinger let out a little giggle, as she tried to lighten the mood.

From Under The Bridge

Mr. Hufflefinger, laughing at his wife's comments, added, "We are all emotionally drained, I believe. It's been quite a day . . . *and* evening! A good rest is what we all need. See you girls soon!"

Matthew waved at Jan and Jenny, smiling as he thought about how great the girls were, and said, "Good night! And thank-you!"

Now it was time for Jan and Jenny (and Jenny's Aunt Vi) to get in the car and go back to their respective homes and rest up, and get prepared for another week of school, as well as for whatever may lie ahead of them.

"It's too bad we couldn't stay and eat some of that meatloaf," Jan said, as Jenny's Aunt Vi drove up to Jan's house. "Mrs. Hufflefnger makes the best meatloaf ever!"

And that made Jenny laugh.

CHAPTER EIGHTEEN

BACK AT THE SCENE

Back at the warehouse, the work was just beginning for Ms. Wright. As she reviewed the case files and the criminal record of Mr. Carter, she was astounded he had been able to remain on the street. His record was long and extensive, peppered by a habit of turning state's evidence in exchange for lesser charges. However, what he had done this time was probably the worst thing he'd ever done, and the absolutely worst set of crimes he had ever committed.

"I wonder if the judge will even accept a plea deal," Ms. Wright thought to herself as she perused the extensive file. "And since there was not only a mass kidnapping, but a bomb threat, I do think Mr. Carter will be imprisoned for a very, very long time."

The bomb squad arrived, just as the SWAT team left. And Ms. Wright and several FBI agents had remained on scene, along with a representative from the Police Department and the Sheriff's Station. This had begun as a cross department venture, and it appeared it would remain that way. As for Ms. Wright, she was happy for the assistance as well as grateful for being allowed to observe and coordinate the effort, as it was right up her alley so to speak.

A bomb sniffing dog began the search for the incendiary device. Ms. Wright, and the lead bomb squad detective, followed a safe distance behind. At the corner window Ms. Wright saw a mobile phone. It was on, and it began to ring.

"Don't go near the device," the bomb squad detective told her. Picking it up, or jut answering it could trigger the bomb. In fact, the ringing may just have triggered the countdown."

"But why?" Ms. Wright asked. "What is the purpose?"

"The purpose is to destroy the evidence."

"Are you certain there even is a bomb?" Ms. Wright asked.

"I'll bet a month's salary on it," the detective told her. "It's' typical."

Ms. Wright shook her head in disbelief, and the bomb sniffing dog ran back to them and lay at the detective's feet.

"That's how he indicates," The detective told her.

"Indicates?" Ms. Wright asked.

"That's how he tells me he has a find," the detective explained to her.

"What do we do now?" Ms. Wright asked.

From Under The Bridge

"We follow the dog," the detective said, as he gave the gesture to catch up to the dog.

The dog led the way to a large cardboard box sitting at the far corner of the warehouse.

The detective kneeled in front of the box and slowly opened it, releasing the center taped shut top with the blade from a small Swiss army penknife he pulled from his pants' side pocket. Inside, he heard the incendiary's device clock ticking.

It appeared Mr. Carter had used his one free call to call his own phone to trigger the bomb, prior to being taken to solitary confinement.

"If we're lucky I'll be able to quickly disarm this thing, the detective told Ms. Wright, as he carefully lifted the ticking bomb from the cardboard box and set it on the ground at his feet

"And if we aren't lucky?" Ms. Wright asked.

"If we aren't lucky, then we'll have to bring in the robot and have the bomb removed to a safe detonation location."

"Could it go off?"

"Anything is possible," he said, as he looked down at the device, still kneeling, and carefully inspecting it. "As the old saying goes, you can fiddle with just about anything and turn it into a bomb," he added with a chuckle.

"And you think this is funny . . . because?" Ms. Wright asked.

From Under The Bridge

"I think it's funny because this is such a simple incendiary device, and it appears the green wire means go and the red wire means stop."

"Is it possible you're wrong?" Ms. Wright asked.

"I'm seldom wrong," the detective told her. "Are you willing to bet your life on me being right?" the detective asked her, as he opened the scissors on the Swiss Army penknife and looked up at her standing above him.

"You only live life once," she said. "So, go for it. It appears the clock is still ticking."

And with a simple cut by a very small pair of scissors, the bomb was disabled. The ticking stopped. Red truly did mean stop.

The only thing left to do now was to gather the evidence, and the sad fact of the matter for Mr. Carter was he had just engaged in a traceable act of attempted double murder. He was certain to spend a very, very long time now in Federal prison.

The rest of the bomb squad either returned to stand-by duty, or were relieved for the night.

CHAPTER NINETEEN

UNDER THE PILLOW

When Mrs. Hufflefinger went into Matthew's bedroom to tuck him in, something she thoroughly enjoyed doing . . . and something Matthew truly needed, she saw something sticking out from under his pillow.

"What's that?" she asked, as Matthew slowly sat up in his bed, allowing Mrs. Hufflefinger to pick up his pillow.

Underneath Matthew's pillow there lay three very sharp knives he had taken from the kitchen.

"Whatever as these for?" Mrs. Hufflefinger asked.

"They're for protection," Matthew told her. "I need these for protection, in case someone comes to take me away during the night so that they can hurt me again."

From Under The Bridge

"Oh, Matthew," Mrs. Wright said. "You don't need those knives under your pillow. Mr. Hufflefinger and I won't ever let anyone come in the middle of the night to take you away and hurt you."

"What if they just take me away?" Matthew pleaded. "I'll need those knives to protect myself, so I can stay here."

"No, you don't. You aren't going to go anywhere."

"Will you just leave me someplace like my mom did?"

"Of course not, Matthew. We love you! And so all of the animals here on the farm! Why, we would be lost without you."

"Can I stay here forever?"

"Of course, you can!"

"That's good," Matthew told Mrs. Hufflefinger. "I really do like it here!"

Just then the family cat entered the room and climbed up on the bed and started purring.

"Kitty would miss you terribly if you weren't here," Mrs. Hufflefinger told him. "And Mr. Hufflefinger needs all the help he can get in the garden . . . and who would help me squeeze the lemons for the lemonade if you weren't here?"

"Matthew smiled.

"Can I stay home from school tomorrow?" he asked. "I'm afraid to go there. I'm afraid someone will take me away," he added as he picked up the knives from under his pillow and handed them to Mrs. Hufflefinger. "I only feel safe here right now."

"Only if you help me bake bread and cookies!" Mrs. Hufflefinger told Matthew with a smile.

That seemed to satisfy Matthew. And (after all) it made sense that he would feel that way, Mrs. Hufflefinger reasoned. A lot had happened, and way too much had happened to Matthew already in his oh so young life.

She kissed Matthew on the forehead, tucked him soundly into bed, and returned to her kitchen with the knives.

"I have a big baking day ahead of me with Matthew," she told Mr. Hufflefinger, who asked no questions.

"Now, don't you let that boy get sick eating too many cookies!" he cajoled.

Mr. Hufflefinger was good at reading between the lines.

CHAPTER TWENTY

A Surprise At School

It was Monday morning and time for Jan and Jenny to get back to school. School seemed so boring to them lately with all the excitement they were having trying to help the kids under the bridge along with their homeless parents! But school was very important too, if they were eventually going to get their dream jobs as a lawyer and court reporter when they graduated from college, and by now there was no question that this was indeed the direction in which they were headed.

Jan and Jenny had some of the same classes in middle school, and one of them was History. Both girls were in this class that day when a school monitor entered the room and gave a note to the teacher. After the monitor left the room, their teacher read the note to himself and then looked up, and stared at Jan and Jenny with a strange

From Under The Bridge

look on his face. The two girls, who happened to be sitting next to each other in this class, looked at each other in bewilderment.

"Jan and Jenny," the teacher announced loudly, "you are wanted immediately in the principal's office! Take this school hall pass," he said, as he quickly filled out a pass from a pad of preprinted passes on his desk where he sat at the front of the room. "And get going, girls! This appears to be very important!"

The rest of the kids in the class started whispering and making comments to one another, speculating that the girls were going to get in trouble. Jan and Jenny had no idea why they were being summoned to the principal's office, but they did as they were told and quickly got up from their desks, grabbed the hall passes, and headed for the principal's office nervous and eager all at the same time, wondering what the principal wanted of them.

They arrived at the office, opened the door, and stepped inside the reception area. Jenny waved the principal's note in the air, that the teacher had handed Jenny as they left class.

"Hi! We are here to see Principal Jackson," Jenny told the receptionist at the front desk. " The note says it's important."

Principal Jackson came out of his office and walked over to Jan and Jenny. He escorted them into his office and had them sit down in the two chairs that sat in front of his desk. Then he sat down in his place across from them.

From Under The Bridge

"I suppose you are wondering what all this is about," Principal Jackson began.

The girls nodded their heads as Principal Jackson continued.

"It has come to my attention that you girls have been involved in some very dangerous activity in an effort to help some homeless children. First, let me say that is to be commended. There should be more people like you, and then maybe we wouldn't have such a large homeless population. I applaud your good works!"

Jan and Jenny smiled, acknowledging the principal's praise.

Then the principal picked up an envelope from his desk and said, "It seems I'm not the only one proud of your efforts in that regard. I'm holding in my hand an envelope with a check inside from an anonymous donor."

Jan and Jenny reached out to one another and squeezed each other's hands, excited to hear more!

"Would you like me to tell you how much it is?" the principal asked, smiling.

"Oh, yes! Yes! Please do!" the girls squealed in unison with excitement in their voices.

Then Principal Jackson took the check out of the envelope, along with a short, handwritten note. He read the note aloud first.

"Dear Jan and Jenny," he began, "I have been following your wonderful, and I might add 'successful' efforts to try to make this world a better place; and because of that, I would like you to put this money toward helping those homeless kids you are now endeavoring to help, and their parents, to live a better, more productive life. Keep up the good work! Anonymous Admirer."

Jan and Jenny were beaming with excitement by this time, waiting to hear the amount of the check they could use to help out the kids and their parents.

As he cleared his throat, the principal happily announced, "I now present to you, Jan and Jenny, a cashier's check in the amount of two million dollars, to be used by you to provide the homeless children, as well as other homeless persons you know about in the area, with a safe place to live, and to help them get back on their feet again. Congratulations on a great job!"

And then Principal Jackson handed them the envelope with the check and the short letter inside,, and began clapping his hands!

"Well done!" he exclaimed. "Well done!"

The only question now was where they should begin. They were, after all, just a couple of kids, even if they were Jan and Jenny!

CHAPTER TWENTY-ONE

THE BEGINNING

It was a good thing history class was the last period of the day, and it was also a good thing Jan and Jenny knew what to do with the money. The only issue that remained was how to do with the money exactly what they needed to do.

The bank was closest to Jenny's house, within a short walking distance; and so Jan called her mother and told her she would be stopping at Jenny's on the way home from school that day, if it was all right with her . . . to which her mother replied that everything was fine with her and to take her time and be safe.

"I don't know about you, Jan, but having a cashier's check for two million dollars in my backpack makes me rather nervous."

"And that's exactly why I told you to put it in your backpack and not mine," Jan laughed.

From Under The Bridge

"Well . . . what should we do next?" Jenny thought aloud.

"Well, we did decide to go to the bank. We can't very well just leave something like that sitting around somewhere," Jan told her.

"My dad's home. He'll know what to do," Jenny said. "And we can call Ms. Wright."

"Let's get to your house and see what your dad says," Jan told Jenny, to which Jenny agreed.

The long and the short of it was that Jan and Jenny and Jenny's father (upon examining the check and the letter in the envelope) headed straight for the bank!

A trust account was immediately opened, and Jenny's father had an attorney meet them shortly thereafter at the bank to open a non-profit corporation for them for the stated purpose of helping the homeless.

The bank president was quite impressed.

"I don't think the money will be in the bank for very long," Jenny's father told the bank manager. There is much work to be done, from what I understand."

"And these young girls did this all by themselves?" the bank manager asked.

"All by themselves," Jenny's father replied.

"Well, not exactly," Jenny interjected.

"Yes," Jan added. "We did have help from Ms. Wright, the FBI and others."

From Under The Bridge

"And the anonymous doner!" Jenny interjected, quickly apologizing for interrupting Jan.

The bank manager shook his head in disbelief.

"I think you girls need to contact Father Joe," Jenny's father interjected. He'll know exactly how to put this money to good use."

To that the girls wholeheartedly agreed. You see, Father Joe was in the business of helping the homeless already; and if anyone would know where to begin, he would most certainly know what to do!

"There's a mission in the valley, not far from the bridge. Maybe the children could stay there while their parents get rehabilitated," Jan said very thoughtfully, as they all left the bank, account now created and the money safe.

"That money is a huge responsibility," Jenny said. "And we are just a couple of ordinary kids . . . "

"Oh, I think you two are far from ordinary," Jenny's father told her as they walked back to the house. "And I think that Father Joe will know exactly what to do."

And after that, when they arrived back at Jenny's house, the girls called both Ms. Wright and the Hufflefingers, and the three of them were beside themselves with joy and excitement upon hearing the news of what had transpired that day.

The girls arranged to meet with Father Joe. The rest is history. The parents who lived in the encampment under the bridge got help

From Under The Bridge

for their addictions, and training so they could be useful members of society. The children from under the bridge were all well cared for while their parents got the help they needed; and because Matthew's mother was nowhere to be found, Mr. and Mrs. Hufflefinger were granted permanent guardianship of Matthew, and Matthew found his safe forever home. And as to Jimmy? Mr. and Mrs. Hufflefinger were also granted permanent guardianship of Jimmy! And Jimmy found his permanent and safe home!

And what happened after that will simply remain a mystery until the future melds into the present. And this is because that is how these things go when it comes to Jan and Jenny!

The future is. and was. and will be forever a mystery until it becomes the present. Because this is how life unfolds.

And as for Mr. Carter? He will never again be free to harm anyone, especially a child.

www.ingramcontent.com/pod-product-compliance
Ingram Content Group UK Ltd.
Pitfield, Milton Keynes, MK11 3LW, UK
UKHW022232230426
12048UKWH00016BA/1210